Pakenham Surname

Ireland: 1600s to 1900s

From Ireland Church Records of Baptism, Marriage and Death

Comprised of Roman Catholic and Church of Ireland Records

From Counties Carlow, Cork, Kerry and Dublin City

Compiled by **Donovan Hurst**

May 2, 2013

Dedication

This work is dedicated to all of those that came before us and shaped our lives to make us the people that we are today.

Table of Contents

Introduction

This is a compilation of individuals who have the surname of Pakenham that lived in the country of Ireland from the 1600s to the 1900s. I have placed each entry into one of four categories: Families, Individual Births/Baptisms, Individual Burials, and Individual Marriages. If a marriage entry primarily concerns an Individual Pakenham whom is female, then I have placed that entry under the category of Individual Marriages. If a marriage entry primarily concerns an Individual Pakenham whom is male, then I have placed that entry under the category of Families. Images of many of these listings are available at http://churchrecords.irishgenealogy.ie/churchrecords/.

To help guide the reader of this work, the format of this book is as follows:

- Main Family Entry (Husband and Wife) (Father and Mother)

    o Child of Main Family Entry, including Spouse(s) when available

        ▪ Grandchild of Main Family Entry, including Spouse(s) when available

        • Great-Grandchild of Main Family Entry, including Spouse(s) when available

(**Bolded Text**) following any entry includes any additional information such as Residence(s), Occupation(s), Signature(s), etc. when available.

Hurst

Some of the fonts used in this work symbolizes Celtic writing. The traditional letters, numbers, and punctuation marks and their Celtic counterparts are as follows:

Traditional Letters (Uppercase & Lowercase)

A a B b C c D d E f G g H h I i J j K k L l M m N n O o P p Q q R r S s T t U u V v W w X x Y y Z z

Celtic Letters (Uppercase & Lowercase)

A a B b C c D ð E e F f G g H h I í J j K k L l M m

N n O o P p Q q R r S s T t U u V v W w X x Y y Z z

Traditional Numbers

1 2 3 4 5 6 7 8 9 10

Celtic Numbers

1 2 3 4 5 6 7 8 9 10

Traditional Punctuation

. , : ' " & - ( )

Celtic Punctuation

. , : ' " & - ( )

Parish Churches

Cork & Ross

(Roman Catholic or RC)

Cork - South Parish and Cork - SS. Peter & Paul Parish.

Dublin (Church of Ireland)

Chapelizod Parish, Clondalkin Parish, Harold's Cross Parish, Leeson Park Parish, Rathmines Parish, Rotunda Chapel Parish, St. Andrew Parish, St. Anne Parish, St. Audoen Parish, St. Barnabas Parish, St. George Parish, St. James Parish, St. Kevin Parish, St. Mark Parish, St. Mary Parish, St. Michan Parish, St. Nicholas Within Parish, St. Nicholas Without Parish, St. Paul Parish, St. Peter Parish, St. Stephen Parish, St. Thomas Parish, and Taney Parish.

Dublin (Roman Catholic or RC)

Harrington Street Parish, Lucan Parish, Rathfarnham Parish, Rathmines Parish, SS. Michael & John Parish, St. Agatha Parish, St. Andrew Parish, St. Audoen Parish, St. Catherine Parish, St. James Parish, St. Joseph Parish, St. Mary Parish, St. Mary, Donnybrook Parish, St. Mary, Haddington Road Parish, St. Mary, Pro Cathedral Parish, St. Michan Parish, and St. Nicholas Parish.

Families

- Daniel Pakenham & Elizabeth Mary Pakenham

Signatures:

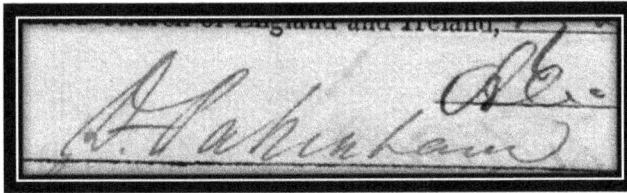

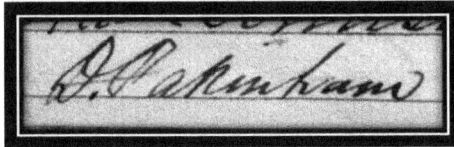

- o John Thomas Pakenham – bapt. 26 Aug 1832 (Baptism, **St. Mary Parish**), bur. 10 May 1833 (Burial,

  St. Mary Parish)

John Thomas Pakenham (son):

Residence - Henry Street - before May 10, 1833

Age at Death - 9 months

- o Thomas Pakenham – bapt. 27 Oct 1833 (Baptism, **St. Mary Parish**)

- o Anne Sophia Pakenham – bapt. 26 Nov 1834 (Baptism, **St. Mary Parish**)

- o John Pakenham – bapt. 24 Jun 1836 (Baptism, **St. Mary Parish**)

- o Elizabeth Mary Pakenham, bapt. 1 Oct 1837 (Baptism, **St. Mary Parish**) & Edward Martin Johnstone

  – 25 Jan 1859 (Marriage, **St. Mary Parish**)

Hurst

Signature:

Signatures (Marriage):

Elizabeth Mary Pakenham (daughter):

    Residence - 57 Henry Street - January 25, 1859

Edward Martin Johnstone, son of Andrew Johnstone (son-in-law):

    Residence - 57 Henry Street - January 25, 1859

    Occupation - Naval Instructor, Royal Navy - January 25, 1859

Andrew Johnstone (father):

Signature:

    Occupation - Esquire

Pakenham Surname Ireland: 1600s to 1900s

Daniel Pakenham (father):

Occupation - Esquire

Wedding Witnesses:

Andrew Johnstone & Daniel Pakenham

Signatures:

○ Frances Pakenham, b. 4 Dec 1838, bapt. 14 Jan 1839 (Baptism, **St. Mary Parish**) & Leonard Kidd –

12 Oct 1859 (Baptism, **St. Mary Parish**)

Signatures:

Frances Pakenham (daughter):

Residence - 57 Henry Street - October 12, 1859

Age at Marriage - minor

Hurst

Leonard Kidd, son of Hugh Kidd (son-in-law):

Residence - 205 Great Brunswick Street - October 12, 1859

Occupation - Assistant Surgeon, 27th Regiment - October 12, 1859

Hugh Kidd (father):

Occupation - Merchant

Daniel Pakenham (father):

Occupation - Apothecary

Wedding Witnesses:

George H. Kidd & John Hodge

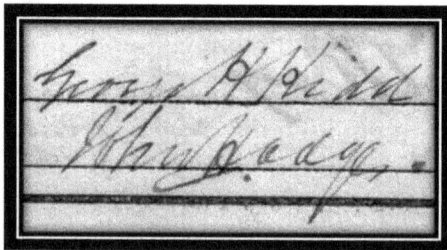

Signatures:

- Francis Fowler Pakenham – b. 11 Apr 1840, bapt. 1 May 1840 (Baptism, St. Mary Parish)

- Isabella Pakenham – b. 10 Jan 1842, bapt. 25 Jan 1842 (Baptism, St. Mary Parish)

- George Daniel Pakenham – b. 12 Aug 1843, bapt. 30 Aug 1843 (Baptism, St. Mary Parish), bur. 30 Jul 1846 (Burial, St. Mary Parish)

George Daniel Pakenham (son):

Residence - Henry Street - before July 30, 1846

Age at Death - 2 years & 11 months

Pakenham Surname Ireland: 1600s to 1900s

- o Joshua Pakenham – b. 19 Jul 1845, bapt. 7 Aug 1845 (Baptism, **St. Mary Parish**)

- o William James Pakenham – b. 8 Jan 1847, bapt. 29 Jan 1847 (Baptism, **St. Mary Parish**)

Daniel Pakenham (father):

Residence - 56 Henry Street - August 26, 1832

January 25, 1842

58 Henry Street - October 27, 1833

November 26, 1834

June 24, 1836

October 1, 1837

January 14, 1839

May 1, 1840

August 30, 1843

August 7, 1845

January 29, 1847

Occupation - Apothecary - August 26, 1832

October 27, 1833

November 26, 1834

June 24, 1836

October 1, 1837

January 14, 1839

Hurst

August 30, 1843

August 7, 1845

Physician & Apothecary - May 1, 1840

January 25, 1842

State Apothecary & Medical Doctor - January 29, 1847

- Edward Pakenham & Catherine Boyle
  - Thomas Pakenham – bapt. 24 Nov 1811 (Baptism, **St. Michan Parish (RC)**)
- Edward Pakenham & Eleanor Gray – 31 Aug 1845 (Marriage, **St. Mary, Pro Cathedral Parish (RC)**)

Wedding Witnesses:

Henry Gray & Julia Champion

- Edward Pakenham & Mary Anne Unknown
  - Edward Pakenham – bapt. 25 Jan 1824 (Baptism, **St. Michan Parish (RC)**)
- Edward Michael Pakenham & Catherine Pakenham
  - Elizabeth Pakenham – bapt. 18 Jul 1769 (Baptism, **St. Mary Parish**)
- Edward Michael Pakenham & Catherine Jane Ponsonby – 25 May 1819 (Marriage, **St. George Parish**)

Signatures:

  - Louisa Augusta Pakenham – bapt. 28 Jun 1821 (Baptism, **St. George Parish**)

Pakenham Surname Ireland: 1600s to 1900s

Edward Michael Pakenham (husband):

Residence - St. George Parish - May 25, 1819

Wedding Witnesses:

E. B. Barker & James Edmiston

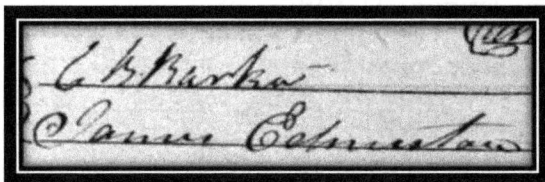

Signatures:

- Graves Pakenham & Mary Swan
  - Georgiana Pakenham – b. 1818, bapt. 1818 (Baptism, **Clondalkin Parish**)

Graves Pakenham (father):

Residence - Leinster Street - 1818

- Gulielmo Pakenham & Mary Travers
  - Gulielmo Frederick Pakenham – b. 16 Feb 1888, bapt. 19 Feb 1888 (Baptism, **St. Joseph Parish** (RC))
  - Henry Joseph Pakenham – b. 31 Mar 1890, bapt. 2 Apr 1890 (Baptism, **St. Joseph Parish** (RC))

Gulielmo Pakenham (father):

Residence - Kimmage Road - February 19, 1888

Kimmage - April 2, 1890

Hurst

- Henry Pakenham & Elizabeth Pakenham

  - Henry Sandford Pakenham – b. 6 Feb 1823, bapt. 3 Mar 1823 (Baptism, **St. George Parish**)

  - William Sandford Pakenham – b. 10 Jan 1826, bapt. 11 Jan 1826 (Baptism, **St. George Parish**)

Henry Pakenham (father):

Residence - Ardbranan, Meath - January 11, 1826

Occupation - Clerk - January 11, 1826

- Hercules Robert Pakenham & Emily Pakenham

  - Emily Pakenham – b. 24 Jul 1818, bapt. 27 Jul 1818 (Baptism, **St. Peter Parish**)

  - David William Pakenham – b. 20 Sep 1819, bapt. 13 Oct 1819 (Baptism, **St. Peter Parish**)

  - Arthur Hercules Pakenham – b. 25 Nov 1824, bapt. 17 Jan 1825 (Baptism, **St. George Parish**)

  - Edmund Powerscourt Pakenham – b. 24 Dec 1837, bapt. 3 Feb 1838 (Baptism, **St. George Parish**)

Hercules Robert Pakenham (father):

Residence - No. 10 Rutland Square - February 3, 1838

Occupation - Honorable Lieutenant Colonel - October 13, 1819

A Major General in the Army - February 3, 1838

- James Pakenham & Anne Ryan

  - Thomas Pakenham – b. 23 Nov 1877, bapt. Nov 1877 (Baptism, **St. Catherine Parish (RC)**)

  - Margaret Mary Pakenham – b. 11 Feb 1882, bapt. 16 Feb 1882 (Baptism, **St. James Parish (RC)**)

  - Ignatius Xavier Pakenham – b. 6 Jan 1895, bapt. 14 Jan 1895 (Baptism, **Rathmines Parish (RC)**)

Pakenham Surname Ireland: 1600s to 1900s

James Pakenham (father):

Residence - Dolphin's Barn - February 16, 1882

35 Cork Street - November 1877

67 Leinster Road - January 14, 1895

- James Pakenham & Catherine King – 3 Feb 1817 (Marriage, **St. Mary, Pro Cathedral Parish (RC)**)

Wedding Witnesses:

Richard Rooney & Joseph Carolan

- James Pakenham & Catherine Maher
  - John Pakenham – b. 5 Dec 1874, bapt. 13 Dec 1874 (Baptism, **St. Joseph Parish (RC)**)
  - Joseph Pakenham – b. 5 Oct 1877, bapt. 7 Oct 1877 (Baptism, **St. Joseph Parish (RC)**)
  - James Pakenham – b. 10 Nov 1879, bapt. 16 Nov 1879 (Baptism, **St. Joseph Parish (RC)**)

James Pakenham (father):

Residence - Kimmage - December 13, 1874

Lower Roundtown - October 7, 1877

Roundtown - November 16, 1879

- James Pakenham & Catherine Warren
  - Thomas Joseph Pakenham – b. 9 Dec 1911, bapt. 17 Dec 1911 (Baptism, **St. Joseph Parish (RC)**)

James Pakenham (father):

Residence - Siberia Lodge, Harold's Cross - December 17, 1911

Hurst

- James Pakenham & Christina Pakenham

  o Jane Miller Ross Pakenham – bapt. 1 Jul 1836 (Baptism, **St. Mary Parish**)

James Pakenham (father):

Residence - 18 Abbey Street - July 1, 1836

Occupation - Wine & Spirit Merchant - July 1, 1836

- James Pakenham & Eleanor Pakenham

  o Frances Matilda Pakenham – b. 20 Feb 1842, bapt. 7 Jul 1843 (Baptism, **St. Mark Parish**)

  o Isabella Maria Pakenham – b. 23 May 1843, bapt. 7 Jul 1843 (Baptism, **St. Mark Parish**)

  o Robert John Pakenham – b. 25 Sep 1844, bapt. 6 Nov 1844 (Baptism, **St. Mark Parish**)

  o Eleanor Pakenham – b. 23 May 1846, bapt. 3 Sep 1852 (Baptism, **St. Peter Parish**)

  o Lydia Anne Pakenham – b. 13 Feb 1848, bapt. 3 Sep 1852 (Baptism, **St. Peter Parish**)

James Pakenham (father):

Residence - 11 D'Olier Street - July 7, 1843

7 Brunswick Street - November 6, 1844

September 3, 1852

Occupation - Painter - July 7, 1843

November 6, 1844

House Painter - September 3, 1852

- James Pakenham & Sarah Unknown

  o James Pakenham – bapt. 1817 (Baptism, **St. Andrew Parish (RC)**)

Pakenham Surname Ireland: 1600s to 1900s

- James J. Pakenham & Elizabeth Monks

  o Thomas Joseph Francis Patrick Pakenham – b. 12 Mar 1895, bapt. 20 Mar 1895 (Baptism, **SS. Michael & John Parish** (RC))

  o Cecelia Elizabeth Pakenham – b. 1896, bapt. 1896 (Baptism, **St. Andrew Parish** (RC))

  o Terence Leo Pakenham – b. 12 May 1899, bapt. 26 May 1899 (Baptism, **Harrington Street Parish** (RC))

James J. Pakenham (father):

Residence - 67 Aungier Street - March 20, 1895

27 Holles Street - 1896

44 South Richmond Street - May 26, 1899

- John Pakenham & Catherine Condron – 24 Jun 1823 (Marriage, **Rathfarnham Parish** (RC))

  o Mary Anne Pakenham – bapt. 9 Sep 1827 (Baptism, **Rathmines Parish** (RC))

  o James Pakenham – bapt. 15 Jan 1840 (Baptism, **Rathmines Parish** (RC))

  o Eleanor Pakenham & James Dunne – 10 Feb 1862 (Marriage, **Rathmines Parish** (RC))

    ▪ Anne Dunne – b. 29 Sep 1862, bapt. 5 Oct 1862 (Baptism, **Rathmines Parish** (RC))

    ▪ Mary E. Dunne – b. 15 Feb 1876, bapt. 20 Feb 1876 (Baptism, **Rathmines Parish** (RC))

Eleanor Pakenham (daughter):

Residence - Rathgar - February 10, 1862

James Dunne, son of James Dunne & Anne Leonard (son-in-law):

Residence - Bray - February 10, 1862

Rathgar - October 5, 1862

Hurst

Sandford - February 20, 1876

Wedding Witnesses:

Gulielmo Murtagh & Sarah Pakenham

- ○ Sarah Pakenham & Bernard (B e r n a r d) Cane – 18 Nov 1872 (Marriage, **Rathmines Parish** (RC))
  - ▪ Bernard (B e r n a r d) Cane & Bridget Kennedy – 7 Jun 1903 (Marriage, **St. Mary, Donnybrook Parish** (RC))

Bernard Cane (son):

Residence - 16 Cullen's Wood, Ranelagh - June 7, 1903

Bridget Kennedy, daughter of John Kennedy & Hannah Keogh (daughter-in-law):

Residence - 10 Smith Cottages - June 7, 1903

Wedding Witnesses:

John Mahoney & Mary Clarke

- ▪ Margaret M. Cane – b. 30 Oct 1874, bapt. 1 Nov 1874 (Baptism, **Rathmines Parish** (RC))
- ▪ James Joseph Cane – b. 21 Feb 1879, bapt. 25 Feb 1879 (Baptism, **Rathmines Parish** (RC))

Sarah Pakenham (daughter):

Residence - Rathgar - November 18, 1872

Bernard Cane, son of Bernard Cane & Catherine Cadell (son-in-law):

Residence - Sandford - November 18, 1872

Cullenswood - November 1, 1874

Cullen Wood - February 25, 1879

Pakenham Surname Ireland: 1600s to 1900s

Wedding Witnesses to the marriage between Sarah Pakenham & Bernard Cane:

Francis Thunder & Julia Malone

Wedding Witnesses to marriage between John Pakenham & Catherine Condron:

Patrick Dunne & Mary Condron

- John Pakenham & Catherine Conroy
  - Sarah Pakenham – bapt. 30 Oct 1836 (Baptism, **Rathmines Parish (RC)**)
- John Pakenham & Catherine Unknown
  - John Pakenham – bapt. 5 Jul 1824 (Baptism, **St. Mary, Pro Cathedral Parish (RC)**)

John Pakenham (father):

Residence - Off Lane - July 5, 1824

- John Pakenham & Elizabeth Pakenham
  - Jemima Pakenham – b. 21 Nov 1852, bapt. 5 Dec 1852 (Baptism, **St. Mark Parish**)

Signature:

  - Elizabeth Pakenham & John Davis – 8 Dec 1870 (Marriage, **St. Peter Parish**)

Signatures:

Hurst

Elizabeth Pakenham (daughter):

Residence - 10 Upper Mercer Street - December 8, 1870

John Davis, son of John Davis (son-in-law):

Residence - 10 Upper Mercer Street - December 8, 1870

Occupation - Saddler - December 8, 1870

John Davis (father):

Occupation - Wheel Wright

John Pakenham (father):

Occupation - Clerk

Wedding Witnesses:

Andrew Plummer & Jemima Pakenham

Signatures:

John Pakenham (father):

Residence - 9 Wentworth Place - December 5, 1852

Occupation - Railway Officer - December 5, 1852

Pakenham Surname Ireland: 1600s to 1900s

- John Pakenham & Ellen Pakenham

  o Margaret Pakenham – b. 29 May 1853, bapt. 6 Jul 1853 (Baptism, **St. Mary, Pro Cathedral Parish (RC)**)

John Pakenham (father):

Residence - 65 Lower Dominick Street - July 6, 1853

- John Pakenham & Ellen Unknown

  o Margaret Pakenham – b. 1 Apr 1853, bapt. 31 Jul 1853 (Baptism, **Taney Parish**)

John Pakenham (father):

Residence - Churchtown - July 31, 1853

Occupation - Laborer - July 31, 1853

- John Pakenham & Unknown

  o William Pakenham, d. bef. 2 Oct 1873 & Elizabeth Fitzpatrick (1st Marriage) – 3 Jun 1849 (Marriage, **Taney Parish**)

William Pakenham (son):

Residence - Churchtown, Taney Parish - June 3, 1849

Occupation - Servant - June 3, 1849

Elizabeth Fitzpatrick, daughter of James Fitzpatrick & Anne Rinkle (daughter-in-law):

Residence - Balally, Taney Parish - June 3, 1849

James Fitzpatrick (father):

Occupation - Farmer

Hurst

John Pakenham (father):

    Occupation - Farmer

Wedding Witnesses:

George Williams & Charles Dodd

- o Elizabeth Fitzpatrick Pakenham (2nd Marriage) & Patrick Field – 2 Oct 1873 (Marriage, **Rathmines Parish (RC)**)

Elizabeth Fitzpatrick Pakenham, daughter of James Fitzpatrick & Anne Rinkle

(daughter-in-law):

Patrick Field, son of Alexander Field & Anne Purcell (son-in-law):

    Residence - Ranelagh - October 2, 1873

Wedding Witnesses:

Charles Howard & Joseph Anderson

- John Pakenham & Unknown
  - o Margaret Pakenham (1st Marriage) & Unknown Howe
  - o Margaret Pakenham Howe (2nd Marriage) & John Brennan – 4 Aug 1858 (Marriage, **St. Peter Parish**)

Signatures:

Pakenham Surname Ireland: 1600s to 1900s

Margaret Pakenham Howe (daughter):

>   Residence - Camden Street - August 4, 1858

>   Relationship Status at 2nd Marriage - widow

John Brennan, son of Fineas Brennan (son-in-law):

>   Residence - 4 Clanbrassil Terrace - August 4, 1858

>   Occupation - Merchant's Clerk - August 4, 1858

Fineas Brennan (father):

>   Occupation - Esquire

John Pakenham (father):

>   Occupation - Esquire

Wedding Witnesses:

William Conway & Richard Thompson

Signatures:

- John Pakenham & Unknown

  o John Pakenham & Hannah Loftus Booth – 26 Jun 1868 (Marriage, **St. Peter Parish**)

Signatures:

John Pakenham (son):

Residence - Lesmolen, Co. Mayo - June 26, 1868

Occupation - Game Keeper - June 26, 1868

Hannah Loftus Booth, daughter of George Loftus Booth (daughter-in-law):

Residence - 17 Heytesbury Street - June 26, 1868

George Loftus Booth (father):

Occupation - Water Bailiff

John Pakenham (father):

Occupation - Game Keeper

Wedding Witnesses:

Edward Pakenham & Edward Booth

Signatures:

Pakenham Surname Ireland: 1600s to 1900s

- Luke Pakenham & Ellen Unknown

  o William Patrick Pakenham – b. 12 Mar 1863, bapt. 13 Mar 1863 (Baptism, **St. Michan Parish (RC)**)

Luke Pakenham (father):

Residence - 7 Bull Lane - March 13, 1863

- Norman (N o r m a n) Pakenham & Helen Ellen Pakenham

  o John Joseph Pakenham & Anne Mary Keary – 25 Apr 1878 (Marriage, **St. Mary, Pro Cathedral Parish (RC)**)

  - Mary Helen Pakenham – b. 15 Jan 1881, bapt. 18 Jan 1881 (Baptism, **St. Agatha Parish (RC)**)

  - Anne Mary Teresa Pakenham – b. 11 Oct 1882, bapt. 17 Oct 1882 (Baptism, **St. Agatha Parish (RC)**)

  - Anne Mary Pakenham – b. 25 Mar 1885, bapt. 27 Mar 1885 (Baptism, **St. Michan Parish (RC)**)

  - John Joseph Pakenham – b. 5 Mar 1887, bapt. 8 Mar 1887 (Baptism, **Unknown Parish, Dublin (RC)**)

  - Joseph Ignatius Pakenham – b. 8 Feb 1889, bapt. 12 Feb 1889 (Baptism, **Unknown Parish, Dublin (RC)**)

  - Alphonse Joseph Pakenham – b. 9 Sep 1890, bapt. 12 Sep 1890 (Baptism, **Harrington Street Parish (RC)**)

John Joseph Pakenham (son):

Residence - 10 Buckingham Place - April 25, 1878

8 Russell Terrace - January 18, 1881

October 17, 1882

24 St. Patrick Road, Drumcondra - March 27, 1885

Hurst

28 Longwood Avenue - March 8, 1887

February 12, 1889

September 12, 1890

Anne Mary Keary, daughter of Arthur Keary & Catherine Unknown (daughter-in-law):

Residence - 32 North Great George's Street - April 25, 1878

Wedding Witnesses:

James Pakenham & Clare O'Brien

- Robert Pakenham & Harriet Mary Browne – 19 Jun 1829 (Marriage, St. George Parish)

Signatures:

Robert Pakenham (husband):

Residence - Albridge Parish, Co. Kildare - June 19, 1829

Occupation - Reverend, Clerk - June 19, 1829

Harriet Mary Browne (wife):

Residence - St. George Parish - June 19, 1829

Wedding Witnesses:

Thomas Abraham, George Browne, & William J. Purdon

Signatures:

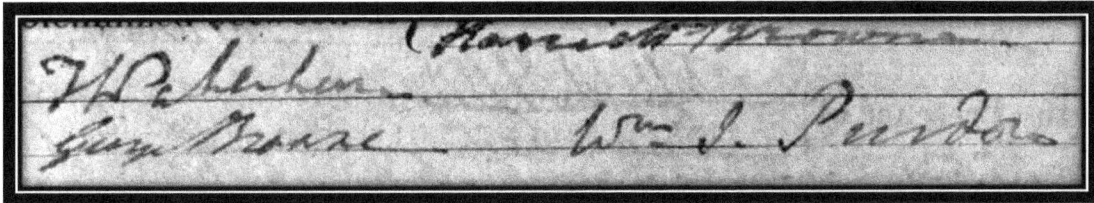

- Robert Pakenham & Jane Unknown

  - Robert Pakenham – bapt. 26 Apr 1795 (Baptism, **St. Audoen Parish**)

- Robert Pakenham & Unknown

  - Unknown Pakenham, d. bef. 22 Jun 1858 & Sarah Jane Mills (1st Marriage)

  - Sarah Jane Mills Pakenham (2nd Marriage) & Francis Baker – 22 Jun 1858 (Marriage, **St. Mary Parish**)

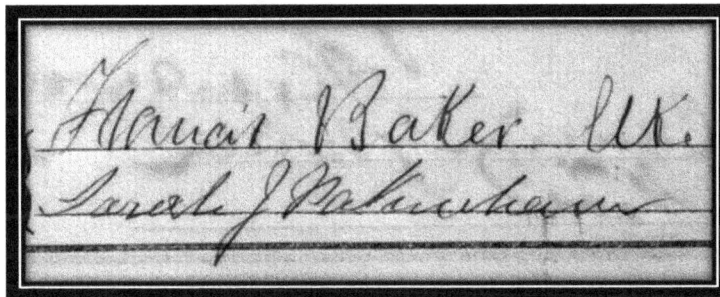

Signatures:

Sarah Jane Mills Pakenham, daughter of William Mills (daughter-in-law):

   Residence - Malheny, Co. Dublin - June 22, 1858

   Relationship Status at 2nd Marriage - widow

Hurst

Francis Baker, son of Francis Baker (son-in-law):

  Residence - 56 Mount Joy Street - June 22, 1858

  Occupation - Clerk in Holy Orders - June 22, 1858

  Relationship Status at Marriage - widow

Francis Baker (father):

  Occupation - Clerk in Holy Orders

William Mills (father):

  Occupation - Barrister

Wedding Witnesses:

Arthur Baker & James Joseph Mills

Signatures:

o   Elizabeth Sophia Pakenham & James Joseph Mills – 25 Feb 1869 (Marriage, St. Mary Parish)

Signature:

Pakenham Surname Ireland: 1600s to 1900s

Signatures (Marriage):

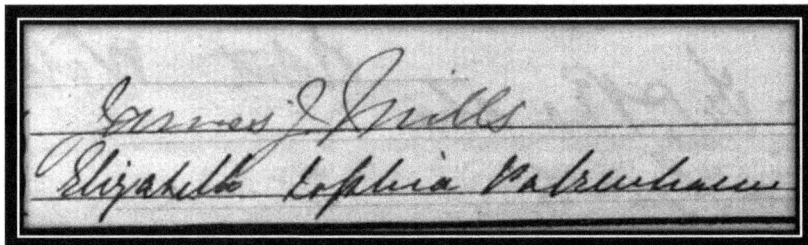

Elizabeth Sophia Pakenham (daughter):

    Residence - 4 Berkley Street - February 25, 1869

James Joseph Mills, son of William Mills (son-in-law):

    Residence - Castle Adder, Yara Parish, Co. Meath - February 25, 1869

    Occupation - Esquire - February 25, 1869

William Mills (father):

    Occupation - Barrister at Law

Robert Pakenham (father):

    Occupation - Clergyman, Establish Church

Wedding Witnesses:

C. Pakenham & Harriet Twine

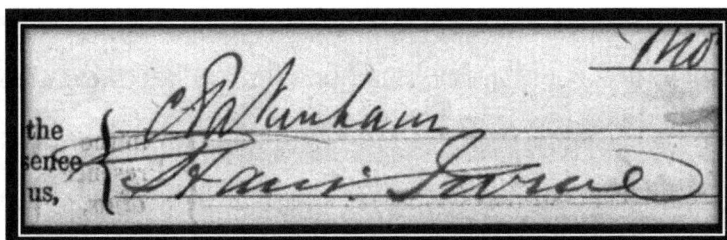

Signatures:

Hurst

- Samuel Pakenham & Sarah Unknown

  - William Pakenham – bapt. 14 Jul 1765 (Baptism, **St. James Parish**)

Samuel Pakenham (father):

Residence - Dolphin's Barn - July 14, 1765

Occupation - Shoemaker - July 14, 1765

- Thomas Pakenham & Anne Nolan – 28 Nov 1841 (Marriage, **St. Peter Parish**)

Thomas Pakenham (husband):

Residence - Crumlin Road - November 28, 1841

Occupation - Gardner - November 28, 1841

Anne Nolan (wife):

Residence - 24 Baggot Street - November 28, 1841

Wedding Witnesses:

John Echlin Bronford & John Vossen

- Thomas Pakenham & Elizabeth Cullen – 15 Oct 1837 (Marriage, **St. Catherine Parish (RC)**)

  - Margaret Pakenham & John Toole – Feb 1864 (Marriage, **St. Catherine Parish (RC)**)

    - Joseph Toole – b. 8 Mar 1865, bapt. 14 Mar 1865 (Baptism, **St. Catherine Parish (RC)**)

    - Thomas Toole – b. 4 Aug 1871, bapt. 8 Aug 1871 (Baptism, **St. Catherine Parish (RC)**)

    - Emily Mary Toole – b. 11 Oct 1874, bapt. 13 Oct 1874 (Baptism, **St. Catherine Parish (RC)**)

    - James Joseph Toole – b. 22 Mar 1876, bapt. Mar 1876 (Baptism, **St. Catherine Parish (RC)**)

    - Patrick Toole – b. 23 Aug 1880, bapt. 30 Aug 1880 (Baptism, **St. Nicholas Parish (RC)**)

    - Emily Mary Toole – b. 28 Apr 1882, bapt. 3 May 1882 (Baptism, **St. Michan Parish (RC)**)

Pakenham Surname Ireland: 1600s to 1900s

Margaret Pakenham (daughter):

    Residence - 38 Cork Street - February 1864

John Toole, son of John Toole & Catherine Unknown (son-in-law):

    Residence - 6 Marrowbone Lane - February 1864

        11 Pimlico Street - March 14, 1865

        4 Browne Street - August 8, 1871

        23 Marrowbone Lane - October 13, 1874

        20 Marrowbone Lane - March 1876

        84 Healy's Place - August 30, 1880

        10 Linen Hall Street - May 3, 1882

Wedding Witnesses:

John Mossan & Elizabeth Pakenham

- Elizabeth Pakenham (1st Marriage) & John Smythe – 1 Feb 1865 (Marriage, **St. Catherine Parish** (RC))

Elizabeth Pakenham (daughter):

    Residence - 38 Cork Street - February 1, 1865

John Smythe, son of Thomas Smythe & Elizabeth Cullen (son-in-law):

    Residence - 38 Cork Street - February 1, 1865

Wedding Witnesses:

John Nangle & Eleanor Dunne

- Elizabeth Pakenham Smythe (2nd Marriage) & Patrick Joseph Lennox – 1 Oct 1894 (Marriage, Rathmines Parish (RC))

Elizabeth Pakenham Smythe (daughter):

Residence - 30 Rathmines Road - October 1, 1894

Patrick Joseph Lennox, son of Thomas Lennox & Mary O'Brien (son-in-law):

Residence - 30 Rathmines Road - October 1, 1894

Wedding Witnesses:

Luke M. Nolan & Anne Lennox

- Amelia Pakenham, bapt. 25 Jan 1850 (Baptism, **St. Catherine Parish (RC)**) & John Whelan – 27 Jul 1870 (Marriage, **St. Catherine Parish (RC)**)
  - Elizabeth Mary Pakenham Whelan – b. 2 Oct 1873, bapt. 7 Oct 1873 (Baptism, **St. Catherine Parish (RC)**)

Amelia Pakenham (daughter):

Residence - 38 Cork Street - July 27, 1870

John Whelan, son of James Whelan & Mary Unknown (son-in-law):

Residence - Arbour Hill - July 27, 1870

38 Cork Street - October 7, 1873

Wedding Witnesses:

Martin Whelan & Bridget Whelan

- o Charles Lawrence Pakenham – b. 13 Apr 1858, bapt. 30 Apr 1858 (Baptism, **St. Catherine Parish** (RC))

- o Charles Reginald Pakenham – b. 21 May 1860, bapt. 8 Jun 1860 (Baptism, **St. Catherine Parish** (RC))

Thomas Pakenham (father):

Residence - 38 Cork Street - April 30, 1858

June 8, 1860

Wedding Witnesses:

Michael Martin & Philip Cullen

- Thomas Pakenham & Elizabeth Unknown
  - o Margaret Pakenham – bapt. 24 Feb 1841 (Baptism, **St. Audoen Parish** (RC))
- Thomas Pakenham & Ellen Wallace
  - o James Pakenham – b. 28 Feb 1859, bapt. 28 Feb 1859 (Baptism, **St. James Parish** (RC))
  - o Thomas Pakenham & Mary Smyth – 20 Jan 1881 (Marriage, **St. Mary, Pro Cathedral Parish** (RC))
    - ▪ Arthur John Joseph Pakenham – b. 28 Oct 1881, bapt. 31 Oct 1881 (Baptism, **St. Mary, Pro Cathedral Parish** (RC))
    - ▪ Ellen Frances Pakenham – b. 5 Jan 1884, bapt. 14 Jan 1884 (Baptism, **St. Mary, Pro Cathedral Parish** (RC))

Thomas Pakenham (son):

Residence - 10 Buckingham Place - January 20, 1881

42 Upper Gloucester Street - October 31, 1881

Hurst

11 Middle Gardiner Street - January 14, 1884

Mary Smyth, daughter of Arthur Smyth & Mary Fox (daughter-in-law):

Residence - 3 Stafford Street - January 20, 1881

Wedding Witnesses:

Francis Deegan & Anne Deegan

Thomas Pakenham (father):

Residence - High Road - February 28, 1859

- Thomas Pakenham & Georgina Pakenham
    - Louisa Elizabeth Pakenham – b. 23 Feb 1830, bapt. 2 Apr 1830 (Baptism, St. George Parish)
    - Francis John Pakenham – b. 29 Feb 1832, bapt. 15 Mar 1832 (Baptism, St. George Parish)

Thomas Pakenham (father):

Residence - No. [Blank] Rutland Square East - April 2, 1830

March 15, 1832

Occupation - Earl of Longford - April 2, 1830

March 15, 1832

Georgina Pakenham (mother):

Occupation - Countess of Longford - April 2, 1830

March 15, 1832

Pakenham Surname Ireland: 1600s to 1900s

- Thomas Pakenham & Mary Billingham – 18 Feb 1696 (Marriage, **St. Michan Parish**)

Thomas Pakenham (husband):

    Title - Sir, Knight

Mary Billingham (wife):

    Residence - St. Michan Parish - February 18, 1696

- Thomas Pakenham & Sarah Jane Johnston – 4 May 1838 (Marriage, **St. George Parish**)

Signatures:

Thomas Pakenham (husband):

    Residence - St. Anne Parish - May 4, 1838

    Occupation - Esquire - May 4, 1838

Sarah Jane Johnston (wife):

    Residence - St. George Parish - May 4, 1838

    Relationship Status at Marriage - widow

Hurst

Wedding Witnesses:

Arthur Robert Dillon & John W. Dillon

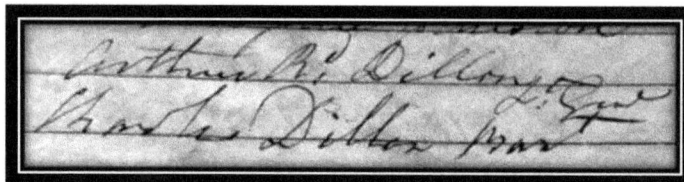

Signatures:

- Thomas Pakenham & Unknown

  o Robert Pakenham – bapt. 16 Nov 1676 (Baptism, **St. Nicholas Within Parish**), bur. 21 Nov 1676

    (Burial, **St. Nicholas Within Parish**)

- Thomas Pakenham & Unknown

  o George Dent Pakenham & Elizabeth Hume – 20 Oct 1853 (Marriage, **St. Anne Parish**)

Signatures:

George Dent Pakenham (son):

    Residence - 12 Upper Merrion Street - October 20, 1853

    Occupation - Lieutenant, 4th Bengal Lancer - October 20, 1853

Elizabeth Hume, daughter of Robert Hume (daughter-in-law):

    Residence - 63 Dawson Street - October 20, 1853

Pakenham Surname Ireland: 1600s to 1900s

Robert Hume (father):

    Occupation - Clerk in Holy Orders

Thomas Pakenham (father):

    Occupation - East India Civil Servant

Wedding Witnesses:

L. H. P. Witherall & W. H. Johnston

Signatures:

- Thomas Pakenham & Unknown
    - Thomas Pakenham & Mary Winifred Nolan – 20 Apr 1897 (Marriage, **St. Thomas Parish**)

Signatures:

        ■ Jane Elizabeth Pakenham – b. 30 Mar 1898, bapt. 24 Apr 1898 (Baptism, **St. George Parish**)

        ■ Unknown Pakenham – b. Unclear, bapt. Unclear (Baptism, **St. Thomas Parish**)

Hurst

Unknown Pakenham (son or daughter):

Remarks about Birth - The church register entry is missing from the beginning of

this entry along with the following entries due to a fire, which

burned the page.

Thomas Pakenham (father):

Residence - 92 Seville Place, Dublin - April 20, 1897

37 Hardwicke Street - April 24, 1898

Occupation - Paper Cutter - April 20, 1897

April 24, 1898

Relationship Status at Marriage - widow

Mary Winifred Nolan, daughter of Thomas Nolan (daughter-in-law):

Residence - 18 Lower Rutland Street, Dublin - April 20, 1897

Thomas Nolan (father):

Occupation - None Listed

Thomas Pakenham (father):

Occupation - Railway Official

Pakenham Surname Ireland: 1600s to 1900s

Wedding Witnesses:

F. Duegan & Jane Cluney

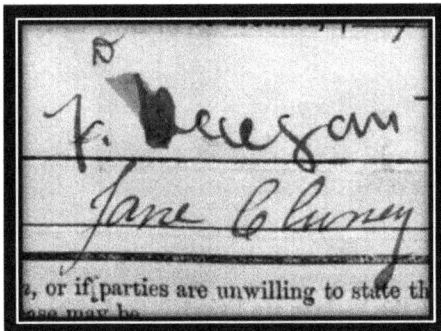

Signatures:

- Unknown Pakenham & Unknown

  o   Unknown Pakenham (Son) – bur. 11 Jun 1676 (Burial, **St. Nicholas Within Parish**)

- Unknown Pakenham & Unknown

  o   B. Pakenham

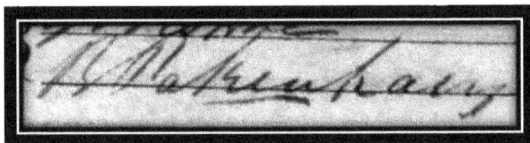

Signature:

- Unknown Pakenham & Unknown

  o   Ellen Pakenham

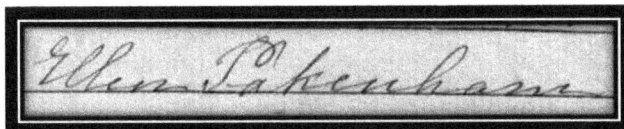

Signature:

- Unknown Pakenham & Unknown

  o Henry Pakenham

Signature:

- Unknown Pakenham & Unknown

  o James Pakenham

Signature:

- Unknown Pakenham & Unknown

  o John Pakenham

Signature:

- Unknown Pakenham & Unknown

  o Mary Anne Pakenham

Signature:

- Unknown Pakenham & Unknown

  o T. H. Pakenham

Signature:

- Unknown Pakenham & Unknown

  o Unknown Pakenham, d. bef. 23 May 1859 & Elizabeth Jones (1st Marriage)

  o Elizabeth Jones Pakenham (2nd Marriage) & John Doyle – 23 May 1859 (Marriage, **St. Andrew Parish**)

Signatures:

- Mary Doyle – b. 10 Aug 1860, bapt. 14 Aug 1860 (Baptism, **SS. Michael & John Parish (RC)**)

- Ellen Doyle – b. 1866, bapt. 1866 (Baptism, **St. Andrew Parish (RC)**)

Elizabeth Jones Pakenham, daughter of Robert Jones (daughter-in-law):

Residence - 5 Trinity Place - May 23, 1859

Relationship Status at 2nd Marriage - widow

John Doyle, son of John Doyle (son-in-law):

Residence - 5 Trinity Place - May 23, 1859

Hurst

7 Longford Street - August 14, 1860

Cliffe Street - 1866

Occupation - Laborer - May 23, 1859

John Doyle (father):

Occupation - Laborer

Robert Jones (father):

Occupation - Gentleman

Wedding Witnesses:

Thomas Moran & Lucy Moran

Signatures:

- Unknown Pakenham & Unknown
  - Unknown Pakenham, d. bef. 19 Aug 1885 & Elizabeth Sarah Whalelaw (1st Marriage)
  - Elizabeth Sarah Whalelaw Pakenham (2nd Marriage) & William Lawder – 19 Aug 1885 (Marriage, Chapelizod Parish)

Elizabeth Sarah Whalelaw, daughter of Robert Whalelaw (daughter-in-law):

Residence - Chapelizod - August 19, 1885

Relationship Status at 2nd Marriage - widow

Pakenham Surname Ireland: 1600s to 1900s

William Lawder, son of Arthur Lawder (son-in-law):

Residence - Northumberland Hotel - August 19, 1885

Occupation - Gentleman - August 19, 1885

Arthur Lawder (father):

Occupation - Gentleman

Robert Whalelaw (father):

Occupation - Gentleman

Wedding Witnesses:

William G. R. F. Gadley & Leonard Lawder

- Unknown Pakenham & Unknown
  - William Pakenham

Signature:

- William Pakenham & Catherine Merriman
  - Sarah Pakenham & William Donohoe – 29 Jun 1881 (Marriage, **St. Mary, Pro Cathedral Parish (RC)**)
    - Bridget A. Donohoe – b. 27 Jul 1884, bapt. 4 Aug 1884 (Baptism, **SS. Michael & John Parish (RC)**)

Hurst

Sarah Pakenham (daughter):

Residence - Graham Hotel - June 29, 1881

William Donohoe, son of John Donohoe & Bridget Kennedy (son-in-law):

Residence - 11 Lower Gloucester Place - June 29, 1881

17 Longford Street - August 4, 1884

Wedding Witnesses:

Thomas Hyland & Margaret McGrath

- William Pakenham & Unknown
  - Thomas Pakenham (1st Marriage) & Margaret Storey, d. bef. 24 May 1882 – 17 Jul 1871 (Marriage, **St. Paul Parish**)

Signatures:

Signatures (Marriage):

- Maude Louisa Alexandra Pakenham – b. 24 Jan 1880, bapt. 5 Feb 1880 (Baptism, **St. Peter Parish**)

Pakenham Surname Ireland: 1600s to 1900s

Thomas Pakenham (son):

    Residence - Royal Barracks - July 17, 1871

        6 Garden Terrace, Upper Clanbrassil Street - February 5, 1880

    Occupation - Lance Corporal, 58th Regiment - July 17, 1871

        Post Office - February 5, 1880

Margaret Storey, daughter of William Storey (daughter-in-law):

    Residence - 6 Wood Lane - July 17, 1871

William Storey (father):

    Occupation - Shop Keeper

William Pakenham (father):

    Occupation - Game Keeper

Wedding Witnesses:

John Harris & Sarah Daniel

Signatures:

39

o Thomas Pakenham (2nd Marriage) & Ellen Wilkin – 24 May 1882 (Marriage, **Rathmines Parish**)

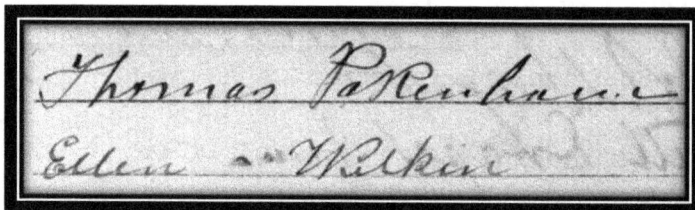

Signatures:

- James Charles Pakenham – b. 23 May 1884, bapt. 11 Jul 1884 (Baptism, **Harold's Cross Parish**)

- John Henry Pakenham, b. 24 Jun 1886, bapt. 30 Jul 1886 (Baptism, **Harold's Cross Parish**) & Bridget Mary Brady – 20 Feb 1912 (Marriage, **Harrington Street Parish** (RC))

John Henry Pakenham (father):

Residence - 18 Olaf Road, Manor Street - February 20, 1912

Bridget Mary Brady, daughter of James Brady & Bridget Craddock (daughter-in-law):

Residence - 2 Daniel Street - February 20, 1912

Wedding Witnesses:

Gulielmo Joseph Forman & Esther Thornbury

- Frederick Thomas Pakenham – b. 8 Nov 1892, bapt. 18 Dec 1892 (Baptism, **St. Kevin Parish**)

- Helen Louisa Pakenham – b. 2 Apr 1894, bapt. 13 May 1894 (Baptism, **St. Kevin Parish**)

- Mabel Pakenham – b. 4 Nov 1897, bapt. 19 Dec 1897 (Baptism, **St. Kevin Parish**)

Thomas Pakenham (son):

Residence - 6 Garden Terrace, Upper Clanbrassil Street - May 24, 1882

No. 15 Liverpool Road - July 11, 1884

Pakenham Surname Ireland: 1600s to 1900s

No. 1 Janeville, Lombard Street - July 30, 1886

December 19, 1897

Janeville, Longwood Avenue - December 18, 1892

1 Laneville, St. Kevin's Parade - May 13, 1894

Occupation - Of Her Majesty's Post Office - May 24, 1884

Letter Carrier - July 11, 1884

July 30, 1886

Postman - December 18, 1892

May 13, 1894

December 19, 1897

Relationship Status at 2nd Marriage - widow

Ellen Wilkin, daughter of James Wilkin (daughter-in-law):

Residence - 135 Leinster Road - May 24, 1884

Occupation - Domestic Servant - May 24, 1884

James Wilkin (father):

Occupation - Farmer

William Pakenham

Occupation - Game Keeper

Hurst

Wedding Witnesses:

Thomas Grant & Mary Grant

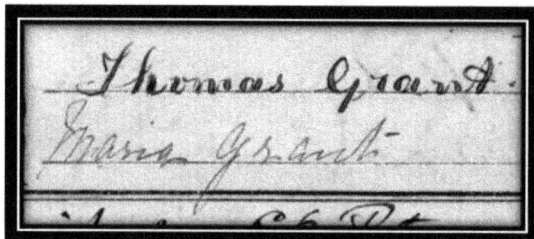

Signatures:

- William Sandford Pakenham & Constance Pakenham

  o Francis Henry Godfrey Pakenham – b. 21 Jan 1865, bapt. 25 Feb 1865 (Baptism, **St. Stephen Parish**)

  o Robert Sandford Pakenham – b. 1 May 1866, bapt. 1 May 1866 (Baptism, **St. Stephen Parish**)

  o Hamilton Richard Pakenham – b. 25 Nov 1867, bapt. 6 Feb 1868 (Baptism, **St. Peter Parish**)

William Sandford Pakenham (father):

Residence - 9 Herbert Street - February 25, 1865

May 1, 1866

40 Harcourt Street - February 6, 1868

Occupation - Barrister - February 25, 1865

May 1, 1866

Barrister at Law - February 6, 1868

Individual Baptisms/Births

- Robert Pakenham – b. 21 Oct 1863, bapt. 27 Oct 1863 (Baptism, **Rotunda Chapel Parish**)

Individual Burials

- Anne Pakenham – b. 1784, bur. 14 May 1856 (Burial, **Taney Parish**)

Anne Pakenham (deceased):

> **Residence - Upper Churchtown - before May 14, 1856**

> **Age at Death - 72 years**

- Anne Pakenham – bur. 28 Dec 1843 (Burial, **Taney Parish**)

Anne Pakenham (deceased):

> **Residence - Churchtown - before December 28, 1843**

- Eleanor Pakenham – b. 1754, bur. 11 Oct 1847 (Burial, **Taney Parish**)

Eleanor Pakenham (deceased):

> **Residence - Churchtown - before October 11, 1847**

> **Age at Death - 93 years**

- Henry Pakenham – bur. 3 Jan 1685 (Burial, **St. Michan Parish**)

Henry Pakenham (deceased):

> **Occupation - Soldier of Captain Forth's Company - before January 3, 1685**

- John Pakenham – b. 1783, bur. 31 Dec 1848 (Burial, **Taney Parish**)

John Pakenham (deceased):

Pakenham Surname Ireland: 1600s to 1900s

Residence - Churchtown - before December 31, 1848

Age at Death - 65 years

- John Pakenham – b. 1843, bur. 31 Jan 1847 (Burial, **Taney Parish**)

John Pakenham (deceased):

Residence - Churchtown - before January 31, 1847

Age at Death - 4 years

- John Pakenham – b. 1847, bur. 15 Jul 1862 (Burial, **Taney Parish**)

John Pakenham (deceased):

Residence - Churchtown - before July 15, 1862

Age at Death - 15 years

- John Pakenham – b. 1809, bur. 8 Dec 1863 (Burial, **Taney Parish**)

John Pakenham (deceased):

Residence - Churchtown - before December 8, 1863

Age at Death - 54 Years

- Thomas Pakenham – bur. 21 Nov 1776 (Burial, **St. Nicholas Without Parish**)

- William Pakenham – b. 1822, bur. 10 Jul 1864 (Burial, **Taney Parish**)

William Pakenham (deceased):

Residence - Churchtown - July 10, 1864

Age at Death - 42 years

Individual Marriages

- Anne Pakenham & Peter Doran – 11 Mar 1800 (Marriage, **Lucan Parish (RC)**) (Marriage, **St. Mary, Haddington Road Parish (RC)**)

Wedding Witnesses:

John Doyle & Martin Breen

- Catherine Pakenham & Joseph Gurnett (G u r n e t t)
  - Mary Josephine Gurnett (G u r n e t t) – b. 29 Sep 1881, bapt. 3 Oct 1881 (Baptism, **St. Mary, Pro Cathedral Parish (RC)**)
  - John Joseph Gurnett (G u r n e t t) – b. 19 Jun 1886, bapt. 21 Jun 1886 (Baptism, **St. Mary, Pro Cathedral Parish (RC)**)

Joseph Gurnett (father):

Residence - 11 Lower Gloucester Place - October 3, 1881

11 Upper Gloucester Street - June 21, 1886

- Charlotte Pakenham & John Quintrill – 28 Oct 1836 (Marriage, **Rathmines Parish (RC)**)
  - Mary Quintrill & Michael Anderson – 24 Oct 1858 (Marriage, **Rathmines Parish (RC)**)

Mary Quintrill (daughter):

Residence - Rathmines - October 24, 1858

Michael Anderson, son of Michael Anderson & Teresa Heffernan (son-in-law):

Residence - Richmond Street - October 24, 1858

Pakenham Surname Ireland: 1600s to 1900s

Wedding Witnesses to marriage between Mary Quintrill & Michael Anderson:

Samuel Cook & Mary Anderson

Wedding Witnesses to marriage between Charlotte Pakenham & John Quintrill:

Thomas O'Neil & Marian McMahon

- Eleanor Pakenham & James Dodd – 4 Nov 1828 (Marriage, **Taney Parish**)

Wedding Witnesses:

John Pagnam & N. O'Neil

- Eleanor Pakenham & Philip Doyle – 16 Jul 1809 (Marriage, **Lucan Parish (RC)**) (Marriage, **St. Mary, Haddington Road Parish (RC)**)
  - Thomas Doyle – bapt. 1818 (Baptism, **St. Mary Parish (RC)**)

Wedding Witnesses:

John Doyle & Martin Breen

- Eleanor Pakenham & William Drayton – 24 Jun 1708 (Marriage, **St. Andrew Parish**)
- Ellen Pakenham & James Dunne
  - Peter Michael Dunne – bapt. 2 Oct 1870 (Baptism, **Cork -South Parish (RC)**)
- Emily Pakenham & Michael Keady
  - Mary Josephine Keady – b. 24 Feb 1882, bapt. 3 Mar 1882 (Baptism, **Unknown Parish, Dublin (RC)**)

Michael Keady (father):

Residence - 34 Lower Clanbrassil Street - March 3, 1882

Hurst

- Helen Pakenham & James Dunne

  o Anne Dunne & Patrick Nolan – 29 Jun 1887 (Marriage, **St. Mary, Donnybrook Parish (RC)**)

Anne Dunne (daughter):

Residence - 2 New Sandford Road - June 29, 1887

Patrick Nolan, son of Michael Nolan & Bridget Smith (son-in-law):

Residence - 4 Collier's Avenue, Collier's Wood - June 29, 1887

Wedding Witnesses:

James Irons & Mary Nolan

- Jane Pakenham & Patrick Cullen – 30 Oct 1854 (Marriage, **SS. Michael & John Parish (RC)**)

  o Stephen Joseph Berd Cullen – b. 26 Dec 1858, bapt. 9 Jan 1859 (Baptism, **Rathmines Parish (RC)**)

Patrick Cullen (father):

Residence - Rathgar - January 9, 1859

Wedding Witnesses:

Christopher McGuinness & Mary Woods

- Margaret Pakenham & James Sullivan – 6 Apr 1880 (Marriage, **Cork -SS. Peter & Paul Parish (RC)**)

Margaret Pakenham (wife):

Residence - 70 Grand Parade - April 6, 1880

James Sullivan (husband):

Residence - Carrigtaul - April 6, 1880

Pakenham Surname Ireland: 1600s to 1900s

Wedding Witnesses:

James Murphy & Catherine Sullivan

- Margaret Pakenham & Patrick Bride

    o Marcella Mary Bride – bapt. 20 Oct 1793 (Baptism, **St. Michan Parish (RC)**)

- Mary Pakenham & Mark Shiel – 28 Aug 1831 (Marriage, **St. Mary, Pro Cathedral Parish (RC)**)

    o Patrick Shiel & Mary Anderson – 4 Aug 1866 (Marriage, **Rathmines Parish (RC)**)

Patrick Shiel (son):

Residence - **Grantham Place** - August 4, 1866

Mary Anderson, daughter of Michael Anderson & Teresa Heffernan (daughter-in-law):

Residence - **Lennox Street** - August 4, 1866

Wedding Witnesses to the marriage between Patrick Shiel & Mary Anderson:

Augustine Anderson & Josephine Anderson

Wedding Witnesses to the marriage between Mary Pakenham & Mark Shiel:

Joseph Kennedy & Ellen Boyce

- Mary Pakenham & William McCarry – 21 Apr 1839 (Marriage, **St. George Parish**)

Signatures:

Hurst

Mary Pakenham (wife):

Residence - 11 Mount Joy Square East, St. George Parish - April 21, 1839

William McCarry (husband):

Residence - Merrion Square East, St. Peter Parish - April 21, 1839

Occupation - Servant - April 21, 1839

Wedding Witnesses:

J. James Barty & Richard Quinn

Signatures:

- Mary Anne Pakenham & Robert Templeton
    - Mary Jane Templeton – b. 1858, bapt. 1858 (Baptism, **St. Andrew Parish (RC)**)

Robert Templeton (father):

Residence - 4 Redmond Hill - 1858

Name Variations

Includes Latin and Abbreviated forms of names found in the original documents.

Abigail = Abigale, Abigall

Anne = Ann, Anna, Annae

Bartholomew = Barth, Bartholmeus, Bartholomeo

Bridget = Birgis, Brigid, Brigida, Bridgit

Catherine = Catharine, Catharina, Catharinae, Catherina, Cath, Catha, Cathae, Cathe, Cathn, Kate

Charles = Carolus, Charls, Chas

Christopher = Christoph

Daniel = Danielem, Danielis

Edmund = Edmond

Edward = Ed, Edwd

Eleanor = Eleo, Eleonora, Elinor, Ellenor

Elizabeth = Betty, Elisa, Elisabeth, Eliz, Eliza, Elizab, Elizh, Elizth

Ellen = Elena, Ellena

Emily = Emilia

Esther = Essie, Ester

Francis = Fransicum

George = Geo, Georg, Georgius

Grace = Gratiae

Gulielmo = Guil, Guillelmi, Gulielmum, Guillelmus, Gulmi

Helen = Helena

Pakenham Surname Ireland: 1600s to 1900s

Honor = Hanora, Honora

James = Jacobi, Jacobus, Jas

Jane = Joanna

Jeanne = Jeannae, Joannae

Joan = Johanna, Joney

John = Jno, Joannem, Joannes, Johannis

Joseph = Jos

Juliana = Julian

Leticia = Letitia, Lettice, Letticia

Lewis = Louis

Luke = Lucas

Margaret = Margarita, Margaritae, Margeret, Marget, Margt

Martha = Marthae

Mary = Maria, My

Mary Anne = Marianna, Marianne, Maryanne

Michael = Michaelis, Michl

Patrick = Pat, Patt, Patk, Patricii, Patricius

Peter = Petri

Richard = Ricardi, Ricardus, Rich, Richd

Robert = Roberti

Rose = Rosa, Rosae

Thomas = Thom, Thomae, Thoms, Thos, Ths

Timothy = Timotheus, Timy

William = Wil, Will, Willm, Wm

Notes

Notes

Notes

Notes

Notes

Notes

Index

A

Births
Alphonse Joseph

About The Author

Donovan Hurst graduated from San Diego State University with a Bachelor of Arts in the major field of studies of History and a minor in the field of studies of Anthropology. He is a current member of The General Society of Mayflower Descendants and has been conducting genealogical research for over 10 years tracing back his ancestors to their ancestral homelands in Denmark, England, France, Germany, Ireland, Norway, and Scotland.

www.ingramcontent.com/pod-product-compliance
Lightning Source LLC
Chambersburg PA
CBHW081200270326
41930CB00014B/3230